THE
NEW YOU
&
THE
HOLY SPIRIT

by Andrew Wommack

2nd Printing 2014

The New You and the Holy Spirit
ISBN 978-1-59548-105-4
Copyright © 2008 by Andrew Wommack Ministries, Inc.
850 Elkton Dr.
Colorado Springs, CO 80907

Published in Partnership
Andrew Wommack Ministries
Colorado Springs, CO 80907

Harrison House Publishers

7 8 9 10 / 22 21 20 19

Item Code: 323

Contents

THE NEW YOU

THE HOLY SPIRIT

THE
NEW YOU

Introduction
Part I

Choosing to receive Jesus Christ as your Lord and Savior is the most important decision you'll ever make. This book will help you understand the choice you've made and discover what's next.

Welcome to the family!

Chapter 1

Understand Your Salvation

When God's Word first comes to you, Satan immediately tries to steal it (Matt.13:19). However, he can only do so if you don't have understanding. That's why you need to comprehend what takes place the moment you accept the Lord. Understanding prevents the devil from talking you out of your salvation benefits.

God's Word promises *"that if thou shalt confess with thy mouth the Lord Jesus, and shalt believe in thine heart that God hath raised him from the dead, thou shalt be saved. For with the heart man believeth unto righteousness; and with the mouth confession is made unto salvation" (Rom. 10:9-10). "For whosoever shall call upon the name of the Lord shall be saved"* (Rom. 10:13).

Have you done this? Have you confessed with your mouth the Lord Jesus? Do you believe in your heart God raised Him from the dead? Are you a "whosoever" who has called on the name of the Lord? If your answer is yes, then you've been saved!

You were saved the very moment you sincerely committed your life to Jesus Christ. The truth of His Word instantly came to pass as you believed in your heart and confessed with your mouth. Congratulations—you've been saved!

God Keeps His Word

You're in good hands now! *"I give unto them eternal life; and they shall never perish, neither shall any man pluck them out of my hand. My Father, which gave them me, is greater than all; and no man is able to pluck them out of my Father's hand"* (John 10:28-29).

Since you've committed your life to Him, He'll keep you. *"For the which cause I also suffer these things: nevertheless I am not ashamed: for I know whom I have believed, and am persuaded that he is able to keep that which I have committed unto him against that day"* (2 Tim. 1:12).

God will be faithful even when you aren't! *"It is a faithful saying: For if we be dead with him, we shall also live with him: If we suffer, we shall also reign with him: if we deny him, he also will deny us: If we believe not, yet he abideth faithful: he cannot deny himself"* (2 Tim. 2:11-13). When you make mistakes or feel discouraged, just remember—God can't deny Himself, because He always keeps His Word!

Knowledge Unlocks Experience

Knowledge from God's Word helps you comprehend what took place in your life at salvation. You began an eternal relationship with the most Wonderful Person in the universe. Knowing and following Him will bring you unspeakable joy. Salvation isn't just going to heaven when you die; God wants you to start experiencing your salvation benefits immediately. This requires knowledge from His Word. As you understand and act on that knowledge, you'll experience the benefits of your salvation.

God has given you everything you need for life and godliness through the knowledge of Him. *"Grace and peace be multiplied unto you through the knowledge of God, and of Jesus our Lord, According as his divine power hath given unto us all things that pertain unto life and godliness, through the knowledge of him that hath called us to glory and virtue: Whereby are given unto us exceeding great and precious promises: that by these ye might be partakers of the divine nature, having escaped the corruption that is in the world through lust"* (2 Pet. 1:2-4). The knowledge of God gives you access to His promises. By believing and acting on them, you'll partake of His divine nature. This means you'll experience all of God's love, joy, peace, health, deliverance, prosperity, and so on that's already in your spirit now by Christ Jesus!

As your thinking changes to line up with your born-again spirit, your life will too. For instance, perhaps you've spent your entire life hating Mondays. You've always given it over to the devil by believing, speaking, and expecting it to be a bad day. Just because you were born again doesn't mean that all of your negative attitudes and thought patterns have changed yet. Monday will be the same as before until knowledge from God's Word causes you to understand and act differently toward it. As the Word changes the way you believe, speak, and expect things to be, you'll start experiencing your salvation benefits—even on Mondays!

Renew Your Mind!

Your whole outlook will change as you grow in the knowledge of God and His promises. This is called "renewing your mind." *"I beseech you therefore, brethren, by the mercies of God, that ye present your bodies a living sacrifice, holy, acceptable unto God, which is your reasonable service. And be not conformed to this world: but be ye transformed by the renewing of your mind, that ye may prove what is that good, and acceptable, and perfect, will of God"* (Rom. 12:1-2).

The way you think must match your born-again spirit. At salvation, your spirit became an entirely new creation. *"Therefore if any man be in Christ, he is a new creature: old things are passed away; behold, all things are become new"* (2 Cor. 5:17). Your born-again spirit is always in agreement with God. The Word will renew your mind to what's already happened in your spirit.

God wants you to think and act like Him! By submitting yourself to His Word, your life will change like a caterpillar transforms into a beautiful butterfly. Don't allow worldly pressure to squeeze you into its ungodly mold; renew your mind. Be transformed by the knowledge of God, and your life will increasingly reflect Christ Jesus.

Your Spirit Changed

Some people don't understand the spiritual nature of the radical change that occurred when they committed their lives to Christ. For example, many individuals receive Jesus in jail because they're desperate for a change. Waking up the next morning, they find themselves in the same cell, wearing the same clothes and eating the same food. They don't feel any different, and their circumstances certainly haven't changed. Discouraged by this lack of immediate outward transformation, they incorrectly conclude that nothing really happened at salvation. Because of this, many never go on to renew their minds and enjoy the benefits of salvation.

Your body and soul (mind, will, and emotions) didn't change at salvation the way your spirit did. If you were fat before being born again, you were fat afterward. If you were bad at math before you got saved, you'll stay bad at math until you increase in learning. Your mind isn't instantly changed; it's your spirit that's been made new!

Since you can't see or touch your spirit, God's Word is the only way you can know what has happened within. *"It is the spirit that quickeneth; the flesh profiteth nothing: the words that I speak unto you, they are spirit, and they are life"* (John 6:63).

Faith is simply trusting what the Word says happened in your spirit more than what you see in the natural.

Trust the Truth

When I accepted the Lord as an eight-year-old, all I experienced was an inward "knowing." A nagging fear of hell left, but other than that, nothing felt different to me. There were no bells, no whistles, nor fireworks. I had to believe God's Word, that said my salvation was true. As I renewed my mind, I increasingly partook of His divine nature and enjoyed living in His promises.

Feelings change, but the truth doesn't! If you genuinely committed your life to the Lord, the truth is He will always honor that commitment. He'll never deny, leave, nor forsake you (Matt.10:32 and Heb. 13:5). Your relationship with God is secure. Whether you felt anything or not, radical change took place in your spirit, and you're now a brand-new person. Trust that God's Word to you is true!

You'll experience your salvation more as you renew your mind. When you think according to the flesh (i.e., what your five senses tell you) and give in to negative external influences, you won't be able to enjoy God's benefits. However, as you trust the truth of God's Word by keeping your mind on the Lord and thinking in line with your born-again spirit, you'll experience God's love, peace, joy, etc. (Gal. 5:22-23). The choice is yours. Begin renewing your mind today!

Chapter 2

Jesus Is Lord

Salvation is God's gift to you through faith in Jesus Christ. *"For the wages of sin is death; but the gift of God is eternal life through Jesus Christ our Lord"* (Rom. 6:23). Salvation can't be earned by any amount of good works, because God doesn't give eternal life based on anything you do. Jesus Christ did everything that needed to be done through His death, burial, and resurrection. You receive eternal life by faith in Him alone!

No one deserves to be saved because of their good works. *"For all have sinned, and come short of the glory of God"* (Rom. 3:23). God doesn't deal with you in proportion to your sin. If you miss heaven by an inch, then you've missed it by a mile. Either you are completely righteous in His sight or you're not. It's that simple! No matter how good you think you are, you've been bad enough to miss heaven!

The Lord explicitly stated that He's not just *a* way to the Father but *the* way! *"Jesus saith unto him, I am the way, the truth, and the life: no man cometh unto the Father, but by me"* (John 14:6). Acts 4:12 declares, *"Neither is there salvation in any other: for there is none other name under heaven given among men, whereby we must be saved."* Either you come to God the Father through faith in His Son Jesus Christ, or you don't come at all!

God in the Flesh

"And when he was gone forth into the way, there came one running, and kneeled to him, and asked him, Good Master, what shall I do that I may inherit eternal life? And Jesus said unto him, Why callest thou me good? there is none good but one, that is, God. Thou knowest the commandments, Do not commit adultery, Do not kill, Do not steal, Do not bear false witness, Defraud not, Honour thy father and mother. And he answered and said unto him, Master, all these have I observed from my youth" (Mark 10:17-20).

A rich young ruler asked Jesus, "What must I do to inherit eternal life?" He wanted to know how he could earn his way into heaven. Notice how the young man called Jesus "Good Master" at first. When the Lord countered him by saying that only God is good, he dropped "Good" and referred to Jesus simply as "Master." By this we know he didn't see Jesus as God.

Jesus Christ was God in the flesh. He wasn't just a good man who gave us a tremendous example of humility and love. He was literally God incarnate! *"And without controversy great is the mystery of godliness: God was manifest in the flesh, justified in the Spirit, seen of angels, preached unto the Gentiles, believed on in the world, received up into glory"* (1 Tim. 3:16).

Either Jesus was a deceiver, or He is who He said He was. No man who claimed to be God—but actually wasn't—should ever be considered "good." However, there's more verifiable historical evidence proving that Jesus Christ lived, died, ***and*** was resurrected than that Julius Caesar ever lived!

Every cult and religion on earth acknowledges Jesus' existence, but they stop short of calling Him God. They'll grant Him the status of a prophet or an inspired teacher sent from God, but not Deity Himself. The rich young ruler did the same by dropping "Good" and simply calling Jesus "Master." He just couldn't bring himself to believe that this Man standing before him was God.

Apart from Jesus being the Son of God, there's no way to the Father! Everything hinges on His divinity. The Lord Himself stated *"that all men should honour the Son, even as they honour the Father. He that honoureth not the Son honoureth not the Father which hath sent him"* (John 5:23). If Jesus wasn't God, then His life wasn't worth more than any other man's life, and He couldn't have atoned for the whole human race. However, since He was God in the flesh, His life was worth more than all mankind—making His sacrifice eternally sufficient for all!

The Great Exchange

Christianity is the only faith with a Savior. All other faiths depend on good works to achieve various degrees of "holiness." The holier you live, the better chance you have of being accepted by that "god." In essence, you become your own savior because "salvation" is based on your own performance. God knew you couldn't live a perfect life! Instead of demanding that you do everything right, He came and took your sin into His own body at the cross (1 Pet. 2:24). He suffered the punishment you deserved, to give you salvation as a gift. Praise God for the Savior!

Jesus took your sin so you could become righteous! *"For he hath made him to be sin for us, who knew no sin; that we might be made the righteousness of God in him"* (2 Cor. 5:21). God put His judgment for sin upon Christ at the cross so you wouldn't have to bear it. Then, when you believed and received the Lord, He placed Jesus' righteousness on you. This is the Great Exchange!

When this exchange takes place, your spirit is immediately re-created with the righteousness of Jesus Christ. You are then able to fellowship with God spirit to Spirit. *"God is a Spirit: and they that worship him must worship him in spirit and in truth"* (John 4:24). Even when you sin, your born-again spirit cannot be contaminated, because of the impenetrable seal of Christ's own Spirit. *"In whom ye also trusted, after that ye heard the word of truth, the gospel of your salvation: in whom also after that ye believed, ye were sealed with that holy Spirit of promise"* (Eph. 1:13). Since the new nature of your spirit is always holy, you can approach God at any time and in any condition. Now that's good news!

Sustained by Faith

The Christian life is both born in faith and sustained by faith. You'll just end up condemning yourself if you try to live it by your own works. As long as you're in your physical body, there'll be times when you fall short. If you're not careful, you'll beat yourself up trying to live right and wonder how God could ever love someone who messes up as much as you.

God's love doesn't change when you make mistakes. If He went to the cross for you as a sinner, how much more does He love you now that you're a Christian! *"But God commendeth his love toward us, in that, while we were yet sinners, Christ died for us. Much more then, being now justified by his blood, we shall be saved from wrath through him. For if, when we were enemies, we were reconciled to God by the death of his Son, much more, being reconciled, we shall be saved by his life"* (Rom. 5:8-10). He loves you more now as a Christian—even when you sin—than He did when you were lost. Don't ever let your failures separate you from God's unfailing love!

The Law's Purpose

God gave the Law to show man he couldn't save himself. The Ten Commandments are really just the tip of the iceberg; there are literally thousands of rules to keep in the Law! Jesus used several of these commandments in an attempt to show the rich young ruler we read about in Mark 10 that he would never be holy enough for eternal life on his own. *"Thou knowest the commandments, Do not commit adultery, Do not kill, Do not steal, Do not bear false witness, Defraud not, Honour thy father and mother"* (Mark 10:19). This young man genuinely thought he could do something to earn eternal life. Doing and receiving by faith are very different from each other indeed!

The Law is like a plate glass window. Whether you break it with a BB or a boulder, it's broken! *"For whosoever shall keep the whole law, and yet offend in one point, he is guilty of all"* (James 2:10). God doesn't tell you to do your best and He'll make up the difference with mercy. Either you live holy and receive eternal life because you earned it (which is not possible), or you receive it by faith as a gift.

This deceived young ruler needed to quit trying and start trusting. In an effort to convince the Lord that he deserved eternal life, he told Jesus that he'd kept all of the commandments since his youth. Impossible! This man's attitude had him going straight to hell!

Loving the young ruler, Jesus tried to bring him out of this deception. *"Then Jesus beholding him loved him, and said unto him, One thing thou lackest: go thy way, sell whatsoever thou hast, and give to the poor, and thou shalt have treasure in heaven: and come, take up the cross, and follow me. And he was sad at that saying, and went away grieved: for he had great possessions"* (Mark 10:21-22). The Lord touched this man's true "god" when He instructed him to sell all of his possessions and give to the poor. The rich young ruler wasn't willing to lay them down and make

Jesus Lord, because he'd broken the very first command:*"Thou shalt have no other gods before me"* (Ex. 20:3).

God is not against you having money, but He's against money having you! Giving away all of your possessions to the poor is not a requirement for salvation. When Zacchaeus, another wealthy man, met Jesus and repented, he declared he'd give half of all he had to the poor (Luke 19:1-9). Jesus never asked this of him, but Zacchaeus volunteered to do it because his heart had changed. The issue Jesus is driving at is who or what do you trust in as your "god"/God?

The Bottom Line

If you believe Jesus Christ was only a good person and that you can get to God through many different ways, you haven't truly made Him Lord of your life. Jesus is either Lord of all, or He isn't Lord at all! You can't receive salvation, which comes only through Him, if you aren't willing to bow your knee and acknowledge Him as God and Supreme Ruler. Either Jesus Christ is your Savior ***and*** Lord or He's not. It's that simple!

Chapter 3

From Death to Life

All people are born into this world separated from God (Ps. 51:5). Adam and Eve died spiritually when they sinned. Even though they didn't die physically right away, their spirits were separated from God and fell under the control of Satan (Gen. 3). Every person born into the earth since then has had this inherent sin nature. *"Wherefore, as by one man sin entered into the world, and death by sin; and so death passed upon all men, for that all have sinned"* (Rom. 5:12).

However, sin isn't imputed until you reach the age of accountability. This means you aren't held responsible for your sin until you're old enough to intentionally violate God's Law (Rom. 7:9). This age varies from person to person, but you need to be born again as soon as possible once you reach it.

A natural birth brought you into this world, but a spiritual birth is required to enter God's kingdom. *"Jesus answered and said unto him, Verily, verily, I say unto thee, Except a man be born again, he cannot see the kingdom of God. Nicodemus saith unto him, How can a man be born when he is old? can he enter the second time into his mother's womb, and be born? Jesus* answered, *Verily, verily, I say unto thee, Except a man be born of water and of the Spirit, he cannot enter into the kingdom of God"* (John 3:3-5).

When you're born again, you pass from death to life. *"Verily, verily, I say unto you, He that heareth my word, and believeth on him that sent me, hath everlasting life, and shall not come into condemnation; but is passed from death unto life"* (John 5:24). At salvation, the sin nature you were born with dies and is replaced with a brand-new, righteous nature. You're no longer a sinner but righteous in Christ!

Never Again!

God's standard of goodness is His own glory. We might have looked good compared to other sinners, but no one is holy compared to Jesus! According to Romans 3:23, **"For all have sinned, and come short of the glory of God."** Who wants to be the best sinner who ever went to hell? We all need a Savior. God declared everyone a sinner, but He loved us and wanted to redeem us. And in doing so, He could declare everyone righteous who has accepted Jesus by faith. Regardless of how bad we were, we instantly became righteous through receiving Christ.

Born-again Christians know they don't deserve salvation based on their own merits. It's only because they put faith in Jesus Christ and His finished work on the cross. All other religions try to approach God based on their personal holiness—what they do for Him. Christians approach God based on a firm heart belief in what He did for us.

All of your sins were forgiven—past, present, and future—the moment you received the Lord. You are now eternally redeemed and have an eternal inheritance (Heb. 9-10). In your spirit, you became sanctified and perfected in God's sight forever. *"To the general assembly and church of the firstborn, which are written in heaven, and to God the Judge of all, and to the spirits of just men made perfect"* (Heb. 12:23). Sin will never be imputed to you (credited to your account) again!

Choose Life!

Even though you're completely forgiven, it matters how you live! You have an Enemy who is committed to your destruction. *"The thief cometh not, but for to steal, and to kill, and to destroy: I am come that they might have life, and that they might have it more abundantly"* (John 10:10). The choices you make determine whether you experience life or death. *"Know ye not, that to whom ye yield yourselves servants to obey, his servants ye are to whom ye obey; whether of sin unto death, or of obedience unto righteousness"* (Rom. 6:16). Yield to sin and you're yielding to the one whose revealed purpose is to steal, kill, and destroy you. Sin gives the devil a foothold in your life, and he'll take full advantage of it!

If you sin, simply repent. God will never leave you nor forsake you. He's already forgiven you, so don't fall for the deception that

He doesn't love you or that you'll lose your salvation. God the Father already rejected and judged Jesus so you wouldn't have to be rejected and judged. Change your mind and turn from the sin. Declare, "Satan, I rebuke you. The blood of Jesus has set me free. Even though I didn't do what was right, you cannot destroy me. God loves me and I choose to follow Him!" This prevents Satan from gaining entrance into your life.

Don't let the devil take advantage of you by you ignoring the way God shows you to live. Renew your mind to His Word, and act on it in faith. The abundant life Jesus provided is yours to enjoy!

For further study, I recommend my teaching *Spirit, Soul & Body.*

Introduction
Part II

Loving God

Now that you're born again, what's next?

God wants to establish some new patterns in your life. By taking the following "first steps" with Him, you'll lay a solid foundation for a growing relationship.

God's love for you won't change whether you do these things or not, but your love for Him will definitely be affected! You've been given the gift of a brand-new life, full of untold potential that's just waiting to be developed. Why settle for anything less than your divine destiny?

Fall deeply in love with God—He's worth it!

Chapter 4

Be Baptized

Every born-again believer should be baptized in water. This isn't in order to be saved but rather because you've been saved. *"Know ye not, that so many of us as were baptized into Jesus Christ were baptized into his death? Therefore we are buried with him by baptism into death: that like as Christ was raised up from the dead by the glory of the Father, even so we also should walk in newness of life"* (Rom. 6:3-4). Water baptism is an act of obedience to God's Word, symbolizing your baptism into the body of Christ.

You were immediately placed into the universal church upon your salvation. As a believer in Christ Jesus, you became part of His eternal body. *"There is one body, and one Spirit, even as ye are called in one hope of your calling; One Lord, one faith, one baptism, One God and Father of all, who is above all, and through all, and in you all"* (Eph. 4:4-6). You became a part of every believer who has ever believed on the Lord Jesus Christ. It doesn't matter if they go to your local church or if they believe exactly the same as you or not. You've been united with all the other believers in the body of Christ!

God's Word commands you to be baptized in water. *"And he said unto them, Go ye into all the world, and preach the gospel to every creature. He that believeth and is baptized shall be saved; but he that believeth not shall be damned"* (Mark 16:15-16). *"Go ye therefore, and teach all nations, baptizing them in the name of the Father, and of the Son, and of the Holy Ghost"* (Matt. 28:19).

Numerous examples from the book of Acts show how the early church spread the Gospel and obeyed this command. On the Day of Pentecost, those who were saved were water baptized (Acts 2:41). Philip water baptized the Ethiopian eunuch and the new converts in Samaria (Acts 8). Thus, the scriptural pattern given for us to follow today is baptism of new believers by immersion in water.

Being "baptized" as a child in a religious system where they sprinkled you with water is not sufficient. Also, you weren't scripturally baptized if it was done prior to your true conversion (i.e., as an infant or young child). The Bible makes it very clear that faith in Jesus is a prerequisite to water baptism (Acts 8:36-37). You must believe first and then be baptized.

A Sign of Salvation

Although water baptism is an important first step in the Christian life, it's not required for salvation. Those who teach that water baptism is necessary to obtain your salvation are basing this on a misinterpretation of Acts 2:38. *"Then Peter said unto them,*

32

Repent, and be baptized every one of you in the name of Jesus Christ for the remission of sins, and ye shall receive the gift of the Holy Ghost." Some say this "proves" you must repent and be baptized for the remission of sins. The key to understanding this verse is the word "for." "For" often means "in order to obtain" but can also be "as a result of; because of; since." This verse says to repent, which means to put your faith in the Lord, and then to prove your faith in Him—as a result of being born again, because you've been born again, since you've been born again—by being water baptized. Those who believe that water baptism is required for salvation also teach that you must live in a system of religious works whereby you earn salvation by personal holiness. This is contrary to what the Word of God teaches.

Water baptism is a sign of salvation. In Acts 10, God told Cornelius, through an angel, to send for Peter in Joppa. When Peter came to Caesarea and began preaching to this man's entire household, they all received the baptism in the Holy Spirit, spoke in tongues, and prophesied. In light of this, Peter asked, *"Can any man forbid water, that these should not be baptized?"* In other words, they were born again, had received the Holy Spirit, and then were baptized in water (Acts 10:44-48). Water baptism symbolized the salvation they had already received.

Holy Spirit Baptism

Once you are born again and water baptized, your very next step should be to receive the power of the Holy Spirit. *"And when he had said this, he breathed on them, and saith unto them, Receive ye the Holy Ghost"* (John 20:22). God doesn't intend for you to live for Him on your own; He wants to live through you by the supernatural power of the Holy Spirit!

Jesus was baptized in the Holy Spirit. *"Now when all the people were baptized, it came to pass, that Jesus also being baptized, and praying, the heaven was opened, And the Holy Ghost descended in a bodily shape like a dove upon him, and a voice came from heaven, which said, Thou art my beloved Son; in thee I am well pleased"* (Luke 3:21-22). *"The Spirit of the Lord is upon me, because he hath anointed me to preach the gospel to the poor; he hath sent me to heal the brokenhearted, to preach deliverance to the captives, and recovering of sight to the blind, to set at liberty them that are bruised, To preach the acceptable year of the Lord"* (Luke 4:18-19). If the Son of God Himself needed the Holy Spirit, how much more do we?

The gift of the Holy Spirit comes to all who ask in faith. *"For every one that asketh receiveth; and he that seeketh findeth; and to him that knocketh it shall be opened. If a son shall ask bread of any of you that is a father, will he give him a stone? or if he ask a fish, will he for a fish give him a serpent? Or if he shall ask an egg, will he offer him a scorpion? If ye then, being evil, know how to give good gifts unto your children: how much more shall your heavenly Father give the Holy Spirit to them that ask him?"* (Luke 11:10-13). Your heavenly Father knows how to give you good gifts. Ask Him in faith and you'll receive the baptism in the Holy Spirit too!

Both Holy Spirit and water baptisms are clearly commanded in the Scriptures. The Lord will lead you into these two acts of faith and obedience as soon as you are born again. Both actions release tremendous benefits into your spiritual life!

For more information about the baptism in the Holy Spirit, please refer to the section of this book entitled, *"The Holy Spirit."*

Chapter 5

Build a Sure Foundation

The Bible is God's Word. He'll give you wisdom and guidance through it. *"As newborn babes, desire the sincere milk of the word, that ye may grow thereby"* (1 Pet. 2:2). As a baby draws sustenance from its mother's breast, so a new believer is nourished by spiritual milk from the Bible. You'll grow as you feed often on God's Word!

God's Word is God-breathed. *"All scripture is given by inspiration of God"* (2 Tim. 3:16). The Bible is charged with the very life of God, and it'll come alive to you as you read it. Through His Word, you'll get to know this awesome, loving God who has saved you. You'll grow in the grace and knowledge of Jesus Christ and become *"thoroughly furnished unto all good works"* (2 Tim. 3:17).

God will speak directly to you through the Bible. *"For the word of God is quick, and powerful, and sharper than any twoedged sword, piercing even to the dividing asunder of soul and spirit, and of the joints and marrow, and is a discerner of the thoughts and intents of the heart"* (Heb. 4:12). Don't just use your head to read this book; come to the Word with an open heart ready to receive from God!

Choose a version of the Bible that's easy to understand. God doesn't want language style to hinder you from getting to know Him. Personally, I use the *King James Version* because it's what I grew up on. However, you may find the old English phrases too difficult to understand. If that's the case, select a Bible to your liking, and read, study, and meditate on what it says. Any version you use is superior to not reading the Bible at all. The Holy Spirit can lead you to other translations later on, but laying a solid foundation of God's Word in your heart is what's most important right now!

God's Word—The Highest Authority

A basic understanding of the Bible is very helpful. I never went to seminary or Bible school, but I studied the Bible sixteen hours a day. It revolutionized my life! Some things I learned right away; others took me many years. But you can never exhaust the depths of God's Word. Everything you need for life and godliness can be found in it.

I wish somebody had explained to me the difference between the Old Covenant (Genesis through Malachi) and the New Covenant (Matthew through Revelation) when I was first saved. It took me a long time to discover that God deals with people totally differently from one covenant to the other. Most Christians see the Bible as one unit, all saying the same thing.

They can't comprehend why the same God shows so much wrath and judgment in the Old Testament and so much grace and mercy in the New. They don't realize how everything changed between God and man once Jesus Christ came to earth. You and I are in the New Covenant in Christ Jesus!

Guidance from mature believers can save you time and painful mistakes, but always check it against God's Word for yourself. Be careful only to receive what's right, because people can steer you in the wrong direction. That's why comparing everything they say with the Bible to see how it matches up is so important. Let go of what doesn't line up, and hold on to what does. God's Word must be the highest authority in your life!

The Word of God is powerful! It's not just a book written by man about God. Some people raise questions about the Bible and say there are many inconsistencies within it. Many good books (called "apologetics") answer these questions and validate the authority of the Bible. The Word is actually a book by God speaking to you through man. All the books in the Bible are supernaturally inspired and have been protected and preserved error free. Your job is to interpret and believe God's Word as it was written. If you do, God Himself will fellowship with you—and that's awesome!

My teaching *A Sure Foundation* will help you understand how important God's Word is to your life.

Join a Local Church

Every step I've mentioned so far—being water baptized, receiving the baptism in the Holy Spirit, building a sure foundation in the Word of God—can be made much easier if you get involved in a good local church.

The Lord created the church, which is simply a group of His people who meet together regularly for the purpose of loving each other, praying for each other, and building each other up. It doesn't always function that way, but it's still the greatest institution on earth!

Many people love the Lord, but don't like His people. That's because some Christians don't reflect God like they should. They hurt others with their mean-spiritedness and hypocrisy. Jesus faced the same thing—unbelievers welcomed Him, while religious folks persecuted Him. Because of this, you may want to commit your life to Christ and enjoy a relationship with Him but have nothing to do with a church. I can relate to what you're feeling, but that's a wrong attitude to keep. It's like fixing a leaky boat—better to be inside making repairs than outside in the ocean where you could drown!

Coals Stay Hot in the Fire

You grow spiritually by participating in a good church. As a believer, you're like a hot coal in a burning fire. You'll stay red hot and glowing as long as you're involved with other believers in a local church body. Separate and isolate yourself from the other coals, and it won't be long before you grow cold. Stay in the fire! Although there are plenty of bad churches out there, it's worth your effort to find the good ones. Every believer needs to be involved in a local church!

You can learn a lot from Christians who have walked in God's Word and have been through some things. It's important not to believe just anyone, but God will place spiritual leaders in your life for the purpose of helping you grow. *"And he gave some, apostles; and some, prophets; and some, evangelists; and some, pastors and teachers; For the perfecting of the saints, for the work of the ministry, for the edifying of the body of Christ"* (Eph. 4:11-12). Many new believers want to bypass people and receive everything they need straight from God. However, the Lord prefers to work through mature Christians to build up and strengthen newer ones.

God uses apostles, prophets, evangelists, pastors, and teachers to equip and mature believers for the work of the ministry. He gave these people to build up the body of Christ until *"we all come in the unity of the faith, and of the knowledge of the Son of God, unto a perfect man, unto the measure of the stature of*

the fulness of Christ" (Eph. 4:13). Since the church hasn't fully attained that yet, God is still using these five different types of ministry gifts to accomplish His goals. It's important that you submit to the Lord's system!

You are disobeying God if you don't get involved with other believers. God will still love you and you won't lose your salvation, but you'll be a cold, isolated coal when you run into hurts and difficult situations. Instead of having a strong support system of other believers who love you and know your situation, you'll be on your own in the ocean. You definitely need to participate in a good church!

Relationship with His People

What you hear while you're young in the Lord will greatly impact your spiritual development. As a new believer, you're like a little plant that needs to be in a protected environment until your roots grow deep. When I was young in my faith, I'd walk out in the middle of a service if I heard something contrary to God's Word being preached. Today, I don't just get up and leave, because I know it won't hurt me the way it would've when I was first born again. However, I don't subject myself to wrong teaching again and again, because it's unwise. If you hear something enough you'll start to believe it. Since you are forming your spiritual root structures, it's crucial that you hear correct teaching now.

Although what you hear as a new believer is important, a church will supply you with more than just teaching. Your participation in a local body can provide you with needed fellowship and relationships with other Christians. Media ministries like mine can feed you God's Word through audio messages, books, websites, radio, and television programs, but nothing helps the Word become flesh in your life better than regular interaction with other on-fire believers!

Christianity is a relationship with God and His people. Before his conversion, Paul (then named Saul) hated Christians. While on his way to Damascus to kill more believers, the Lord appeared to him in a blinding flash of light (Acts 9:1-5). Jesus asked, "Why are you persecuting Me?" Notice that His question wasn't, "Why are you persecuting My people?" That's because the Lord becomes one with every individual who puts his or her faith in Him! If someone touches you, they touch the apple of God's eye. God loves you the same as He loves every other Christian!

God demonstrates His love through His people. *"By this shall all men know that ye are my disciples, if ye have love one to another"* (John 13:35). *"If a man say, I love God, and hateth his brother, he is a liar: for he that loveth not his brother whom he hath seen, how can he love God whom he hath not seen"* (1 John 4:20). No one who refuses to relate to God's people can say they truly have a relationship with God.

Put His Word into Practice

A local church will provide you with the opportunity to put

44

Christ's teachings into practice. It's one thing to hear the Word say to do unto others as you would have them do unto you (Matt. 7:12), but it's quite another to actually live it. Your rate of maturity will slow down if all you ever do is shut yourself up with a Bible for weeks and months. Some things you'll never really learn until you have to deal with other people. From God's perspective, you don't really know something from His Word until you've put it into practice!

Your local church leadership can provide ministry to you and your loved ones in practical ways that a media/traveling ministry cannot. I can teach you God's Word concerning healing, but I won't be available when you need to *"call for the elders of the church"* (James 5:14) to come over to your house and anoint the sick. However, the leaders of your local church can do that and so much more! They can officiate weddings, perform funerals, minister to your children, advise you from the Word, pray about specific situations, and serve as godly role models you can personally interact with on a regular basis. Your entire household will benefit from your participation in a local church!

You'll also find like-minded believers with whom you can establish close friendships. The two most important influences in your life are what you hear/read and the person(s) you spend your time with. This doesn't mean you reject people who aren't believers, but from now on, your strongest friendships should be with other Christians (2 Cor. 6:14-18). If you remain unequally yoked with an unbeliever, sooner or later that person will negatively affect you. *"He that walketh with wise men shall be wise: but a companion of fools shall be destroyed"* (Prov.13:20). You always rise or sink to the level of your closest friends!

Regularly meeting together with other believers protects and promotes your spiritual health. *"Let us hold fast the profession of our faith without wavering; (for he is faithful that promised;) And let us consider one another to provoke unto love and to good works: Not forsaking the assembling of ourselves together, as the manner of some is; but exhorting one another: and so much the more, as ye see the day approaching"* (Heb. 10:23-25). Plug yourself into a good local church!

Find a Good Church

Don't let minor doctrinal issues prevent you from settling into a good church. If the differences are just some external matters and not core beliefs, I suggest you stay involved. Even if it's not a strong faith-teaching church, it's better to participate in some local church than not to participate at all. There are other important benefits you can gain from participating. If you live in an area where you have a choice, always choose a church that preaches the whole counsel of God!

A good church preaches everything God offers in His Word—salvation, baptism in the Holy Spirit, the gifts of the Spirit, healing, deliverance, and prosperity! The denomination I grew up in centered all of the preaching on just the forgiveness of sins. Many people (like me) got saved, but they didn't believe that God's miraculous power was for today. When my father (a leader in that church) became seriously ill, my family and I didn't know how to receive healing from the Lord. No one in our church had faith for it, because we were never taught healing from God's Word. My father died at 54 years of age, leaving me fatherless at 12 and my mother a widow at 38. Much pain came into our lives as a result of this. Our church didn't cause this problem, but it sure didn't equip us to overcome it either!

Be part of a church that teaches the whole counsel of God. Don't stay somewhere that's against the baptism in the Holy Spirit, the gifts of the Holy Spirit, healing, and so on. Having your name on a pew or your aunt as the choir director won't help when you're sick. Although you're personally aware that God heals, you'll be frustrated when you have trouble receiving it, because you don't know God's Word. To receive prosperity, deliverance, or whatever, you need to be taught God's Word. Be part of a church you can wholeheartedly support!

A good church preaches faith and grace for the entire Christian life, not just forgiveness of your sins. Many groups teach that all you need to do to initially receive is believe, but that after you're saved, everything is based on your performance. That's wrong! You don't have to earn God's favor, earn answers to prayer, earn God's love, earn your healing, or earn anything else. Everything God gives you is by grace through faith!

The atmosphere ought to encourage healthy relationships. The pastor should set the tone by being a loving person. It's not necessarily better to go to a big church or a small one. Some big churches have small groups for the purpose of nurturing and maturing believers. Often, small churches naturally have an environment conducive to building friendships and spiritual growth. Whether big or small, your experience in a church will normally come down to the quality of your relationships there.

Trust the Lord to lead you to a good local church. Pray. Then take some steps of faith. It's His good pleasure to guide you to your place in His body!

Chapter 7

Know Him Intimately

God saved you for the purpose of enjoying an intimate relationship with Him from now on! Salvation isn't just "insurance" from hell's flames. Neither does God intend that you receive forgiveness for your sins and then merely survive until heaven. Salvation is so much more! *"For God so loved the world, that he gave his only begotten Son, that whosoever believeth in him should not perish, but have everlasting life"* (John 3:16). *"And this is life eternal, that they might know thee the only true God, and Jesus Christ, whom thou hast sent"* (John 17:3). Salvation is getting to know this awesome, wonderful, loving God for the rest of eternity!

Jesus came to give you eternal life. The idea that salvation is merely "fire insurance" came from the church putting a period where the Bible only has a comma. It's not *"For God so loved the world, that he gave his only begotten Son, that whosoever believeth in him should not perish"* period. So many preachers stop here and emphasize salvation's byproduct of missing hell and totally ignore God's primary purpose—*"but have everlasting life."* You were saved for intimate relationship with your heavenly Father and His Son!

Jesus came because He loved you! He didn't come as a dutiful Creator under some sense of obligation to rescue His wayward creation. Christ's motivation was pure love, and anyone who loves has a need to be loved in return! God's compassion for you in your lost condition and His passion to restore you to fellowship with Him was combined into a sacrificial love that endured the cross. With the barrier of sin forever removed, you've been freed to receive His love and to love Him in return!

The relationship Adam and Eve lost has now been restored to you. *"Who gave himself for our sins, that he might deliver us from this present evil world, according to the will of God and our Father"* (Gal. 1:4). Jesus didn't just save you from a future evil world (hell); He also delivered you from this present evil world, according to the Father's will. You are now able to walk and talk with Him!

Get to know God! *"Thou wilt shew me the path of life: in thy presence is fulness of joy; at thy right hand there are pleasures for evermore"* (Ps. 16:11). *"Jesus Christ: Whom having not seen, ye love; in whom, though now ye see him not, yet believing, ye rejoice with joy unspeakable and full of glory"* (1 Pet. 1:7-8). True joy and happiness in this life come from your intimacy with God. Knowing Him is eternal life!

Follow Me

Become a disciple of the Lord Jesus Christ! A "disciple" is a learner, someone who follows another. *"If ye continue in my word, then are ye my disciples indeed; And ye shall know the truth, and the truth shall make you free"* (John 8:31-32). Learn what God's Word says, and do what He instructs you to do. As you step out in faith to follow Jesus, the freedom in your life will increase more and more!

Your heart attitude should be, *Lord, I know You love me, and I love You too. Show me what to do and I'll do it! I follow You!* Lay everything out before Him, and make no reservations. Recognize that He is God and you're not. Hold nothing back from Him, because He's already given you everything—He laid down His very life for you!

The truth shall make you free. *"Thy word is truth"* (John 17:17). It's only the Word you know and follow that makes you free. You can carry your Bible under your arm and set it beside your bed, but until you put His Word in your heart, it won't do you any good. Meditate (chew on) His Word until it becomes a part of you. Once you believe it to the point of taking action, you'll know the Word intimately. When this knowledge comes, it'll set you free!

I strongly suggest you get my teaching "Eternal Life." It expounds much more on your relationship with the Lord.

You've Chosen Wisely

Welcome to God's family! If you take to heart what I've shared with you and do it, you'll be well on your way to maturity.

I've included for you a helpful list of my teaching materials available that discuss in much greater detail many of the topics I touched on in this book (see "Recommended Materials" in the back of the book). God will use them to further deepen your roots and strengthen your foundation. I strongly encourage you to get ahold of them as soon as possible!

Choosing to make the Lord Jesus Christ the center of your life is the greatest decision you'll ever make! I congratulate you for choosing wisely. As your brother in Christ, I wish to leave you with this word from God our Father: *"But grow in grace, and in the knowledge of our Lord and Saviour Jesus Christ. To him be glory both now and for ever. Amen"* (2 Pet. 3:18).

THE
HOLY SPIRIT

Introduction

Millions of Christians today have received God's power into their lives through the separate, distinct experience called "the baptism in the Holy Spirit." Wherever you go in the world—Africa, Asia, Europe, North or South America, Australia—these believers are aggressively and effectively advancing the kingdom of God!

I grew up being told that God's miraculous power had ceased on earth with the passing of the early church. This led me to believe that I had received all of the Holy Spirit I could get at salvation. After being saved for many years, I became frustrated with my powerless, defeated Christian life. In desperation, I sought the Lord with all my heart and stumbled into the baptism in the Holy Spirit. This powerful encounter with God revolutionized my entire life!

Today, over thirty-five years later, my relationship with the Lord is deeper and stronger than ever. I regularly see miracles of every kind, and my teaching ministry literally reaches around the world. None of this would have been possible apart from the supernatural power of the Holy Spirit!

Whether you are newly born again or have been saved for many years, God's Word clearly reveals that the baptism in the Holy Spirit is necessary, standard equipment for living a fruitful and fulfilled Christian life. The Lord Himself commanded: *"Receive ye the Holy Ghost"* (John 20:22). I encourage you to do so today!

Chapter 1

Empowered Lives

I was born again at eight years old. Our pastor had preached a message on hell in church that morning. Even though I hadn't done many terrible things in my young life, I recognized that I had sinned and fallen short of the glory of God. I knew "hell" was a place where people who didn't accept Jesus as their Lord and Savior went. This concerned me, so I asked my father about it. He explained God's holiness and how sin separated me from Him. He also told me how God's justice demanded that I go to hell. Then Dad made it clear that Jesus came to forgive my sin and suffer the punishment in my place. I remember praying with my father to receive the Lord right there in my bedroom. Immediately, I felt an inner release as peace flooded my heart.

The next day at school, my friends noticed the change in me before I'd told anyone of my conversion. "What's different with you?" they asked. When I answered that I'd been born again, they immediately started making fun of me for being a Christian. Although these classmates recognized an initial difference at my conversion, subsequent evidence of my faith in Christ was meager at best.

My closest friend from grade school never knew I was a Christian until he saw me recently on television. He'd just gone through an extremely difficult time in life and had reached out to receive the Lord from the absolute end of his rope. While visiting with each other for the first time in over thirty years, he was totally shocked to discover that I'd been a Christian the whole time we were friends together growing up!

My faith simply didn't affect anyone else's life! I prayed six months straight for my father to be healed, but nothing happened. He died when I was twelve. Although I easily overcame temptations others yielded to, the tangible demonstrations of God's power described of believers in the Bible were noticeably absent from my life. Basically, Christianity to me was just the doctrines and beliefs I held inside.

Then on March 23, 1968, I received the baptism in the Holy Spirit! Something within me exploded, and my understanding of God immediately shot through the roof. It took many years of renewing my mind before I was able to explain to others the things I instantly knew in my spirit. In fact, my mother thought I'd lost my mind, because of the sudden, radical, outward transformation of my soul, my thinking, and my actions. My intense, new zeal for God, coupled with a lack of wisdom, even got me kicked out of a few churches. I'd become a fanatic overnight!

You never would've heard of me if I hadn't been baptized in the Holy Spirit! I would have maintained my nominal salvation, surviving until heaven and making practically no eternal impact here on earth. This prior lack of victory and outward manifestation of God's power isn't unique only to me. I've read many, many testimonies of people who experienced the same thing—even in the Bible!

Like a Dove

Jesus Himself did not manifest the power of God until He had been baptized in the Holy Spirit. Angels pronounced Him Lord at His birth, but nothing that typified Christ's ministry— preaching, healing, casting out demons—occurred before the Holy Spirit descended upon Him like a dove. *"And Jesus, when he was baptized, went up straightway out of the water: and, lo, the heavens were opened unto him, and he saw the Spirit of God descending like a dove, and lighting upon him: And lo a voice from heaven, saying, This is my beloved Son, in whom I am well pleased"* (Matt. 3:16-17). The baptism in the Holy Spirit served as the turning point from natural to supernatural in Christ's life.

Jesus immediately began His ministry after being anointed with the Holy Spirit. The Spirit led Him into the wilderness to confront the devil (Luke 4:1-13). He emerged victorious and then boldly declared in the synagogue of His hometown, *"The Spirit of the Lord is upon me, because he hath anointed me to preach the gospel to the poor; he hath sent me to heal the brokenhearted, to preach deliverance to the captives, and recovering of sight to the blind, to set at liberty them that are bruised, To preach the acceptable year of the Lord"* (Luke 4:18-19). From this point forward, Jesus did what He was anointed to do!

Many times, the Lord admitted His total dependence upon the Father and the Spirit. He did His Father's will as the power of the Holy Spirit flowed in and through Him. Father, Son, and Holy Spirit always worked together in complete cooperation. As a part of this interdependent, triune Godhead, Jesus would not and could not do any miracles until the Holy Spirit had come upon Him.

God never does anything independent of His Spirit. Therefore, welcoming the Holy Spirit into your life is absolutely essential for you to experience the victory and abundance God has provided. If the sinless Son of God had to be baptized in the Holy Spirit before beginning His ministry, how can anyone presume to be an effective Christian without it?

Ruckus in the Temple

The disciples were spineless wimps before receiving the baptism in the Holy Spirit. These men had followed Jesus for three and a half years, observing His miracles, hearing His teaching, and experiencing everyday life with Him. They exhibited weakness, immaturity, carnal-mindedness, and strife. Upon Jesus' arrest, all their promises to stay with Him—to death if need be—went right out the window. They forsook Him and fled for their lives in terror!

Peter denied Jesus three different times just hours after pledging his "undying allegiance." His natural strength wilted before a damsel, the high priest's maid, and certain others as they each successively asked, "Aren't you one of Jesus' disciples?" Swearing and taking oaths, he answered, "No, I don't even know the Man!" Peter wept bitterly when he realized what he'd done. He hadn't wanted to deny Christ, but in his own human strength, he was powerless not to do so (Matt. 26:69-75).

Then Peter and the other disciples were baptized in the Holy Spirit. *"And when the day of Pentecost was fully come, they were all with one accord in one place. And suddenly there came a sound from heaven as of a rushing mighty wind...And they were all filled with the Holy Ghost"* (Acts 2:1-2 and 4). They instantly transformed into powerful witnesses and testified of Jesus with great boldness. Three thousand were saved and water baptized that first day alone (Acts 2:41)!

Shortly thereafter, Peter and John healed a lame man in front of the temple and caused such a ruckus preaching the Gospel that the religious leaders threw them in jail (Acts 3-4:3). Thousands more believed their message, so the leaders interrogated Peter and John to find out what was going on. *"And it came to pass on the morrow, that their rulers, and elders, and scribes, And Annas the high priest, and Caiaphas, and John, and Alexander, and as many as were of the kindred of the high priest, were gathered togethor at Jerusalem. And when they had set them in the midst, they asked, By what power, or by what name, have ye done this?"* (Acts 4:5-7).

Peter boldly confronted the same men who had crucified Jesus! *"Then Peter, filled with the Holy Ghost, said unto them, Ye rulers of the people, and elders of Israel, If we this day be examined of the good deed done to the impotent man, by what means he is made whole; Be it known unto you all, and to all the people of Israel, that by the name of Jesus Christ of Nazareth, whom ye crucified, whom God raised from the dead, even by him doth this man stand here before you whole. This is the stone which was set at nought of you builders, which is become the head of the corner. Neither is there salvation in any other: for there is none other name under heaven given among men, whereby we must be saved"* (Acts 4:8-12). Peter publicly declared to the entire Jewish leadership that belief in the God of Abraham alone was insufficient for salvation. He clearly told them to believe on the name of Jesus Christ, whom they themselves had killed, or face eternal damnation. Peter left them no avenue of escape: Either accept Jesus or reject Him!

The same men from whom the disciples once fled were now backing down in the face of the disciples' inspired boldness: *"Now when they saw the boldness of Peter and John, and perceived that they were unlearned and ignorant men, they marvelled; and they took knowledge of them, that they had been with Jesus. And beholding the man which was healed standing with them, they could say nothing against it"* (Acts 4:13-14). The miracle worked by the disciples completely silenced the religious leaders' opposition. What a difference the baptism in the Holy Spirit makes!

Clear Instructions

Our Lord's last words to His followers before ascending were clear instructions regarding the Holy Spirit. If your work on earth was done and you were about to turn your entire kingdom over to a small group of people, your last words to them would be very important.

Jesus commanded His disciples not to do anything until they had been baptized in the Holy Spirit. *"And, being assembled together with them, commanded them that they should not depart from Jerusalem, but wait for the promise of the Father, which, saith he, ye have heard of me. For John truly baptized with water; but ye shall be baptized with the Holy Ghost not many days hence... But ye shall receive power, after that the Holy Ghost is come upon you: and ye shall be witnesses unto me both in Jerusalem, and in all Judea, and in Samaria, and unto the uttermost part of the earth. And when he had spoken these things, while they beheld, he was taken up; and a cloud received him out of their sight"* (Acts 1:4-5 and 8-9).

Think about how difficult this must have been for the disciples! Jesus had preached God's Word and demonstrated His power on earth like no one ever before. Due to this, the religious leaders had Him killed and buried. To their natural minds, it appeared that Jesus had been just another man. Yet three days later, He arose from the dead exactly as He prophesied, validating everything He had said. As if that wasn't enough, Jesus spent forty more days on the earth teaching His followers before they personally watched Him ascend to His Father in heaven. These disciples had incredibly good news—news worth shouting from the rooftops—but Jesus commanded them to sit on it temporarily! Why? They needed the baptism in the Holy Spirit!

It's absolutely wonderful to be born again and forgiven of your sins, but you won't be an effective witness until you have the fullness of the Holy Spirit. When He comes, you'll be able to live in victory and testify in power. The Holy Spirit enables you to more fully experience your salvation and to effectively share with others the awesome things God has done for you!

Many Christians sincerely love God, but they serve Him in their own power, because they haven't been baptized in His Spirit. This results in deadness. *"Who also hath made us able ministers of the new testament; not of the letter, but of the spirit: for the letter killeth, but the spirit giveth life"* (2 Cor. 3:6). When believers try to minister out of their own carnal knowledge and ability—even when they say and do the right thing—it just doesn't carry any spiritual weight. So much of the deadness in the church today stems from believers attempting to minister without Holy Spirit empowerment.

Jesus Christ Himself testifies and ministers His life through Holy Spirit-empowered witnesses. Your Spirit-energized words and deeds will carry weight to positively impact other people's lives for the kingdom of God. The Holy Spirit is the One who will help you experience the promised life of victory and abundance. If both Jesus and the early believers needed to be baptized in the

Holy Spirit in order to live powerful Christian lives, so do you and I today!

Chapter 2

Baptized in the Holy Spirit

If you believe the Word of God, you cannot dispute the existence of a "baptism in the Holy Spirit." Speaking of Jesus, John the Baptist said, *"I indeed baptize you with water unto repentance: but he that cometh after me is mightier than I, whose shoes I am not worthy to bear: he shall baptize you with the Holy Ghost, and with fire"* (Matt. 3:11). Christ was baptized in the Holy Spirit (Matt. 3:16, Mark 1:10, and Luke 3:22). The early apostles, including Paul, were baptized in the Holy Spirit (Acts 2:1-4 and 9:17-18). Whenever people were born again in the book of Acts, they also received the baptism in the Holy Spirit soon thereafter.

Many Christians claim that the baptism in the Holy Spirit comes automatically at salvation. *"No man can come to me, except the Father which hath sent me draw him: and I will raise him up at the last day"* (John 6:44). They recognize the Spirit's work in drawing people to God and assume that they get all of the Holy Spirit they can the moment they're born again. Although it's true they have the Holy Spirit once they're saved, that doesn't mean they've been baptized in Him!

Rivers of Living Water

It's one thing to have the Holy Spirit and quite another for the Holy Spirit to have you! There are major differences between having the Holy Spirit present in your life and having the Holy Spirit in control of your life. Spiritually speaking, it's night and day.

Jesus told His disciples, *"And I will pray the Father, and he shall give you another Comforter, that he may abide with you for ever; Even the Spirit of truth; whom the world cannot receive, because it seeth him not, neither knoweth him: but ye know him; for he dwelleth with you, and shall be in you"* (John 14:16-17).

Prior to Jesus' resurrection, the Holy Spirit couldn't be received the way we are discussing. He was present **with** the disciples and worked through them (as evidenced by the miracles they did), but He wasn't **in** them. This was because the fullness of the Holy Spirit couldn't be received until after Christ had ascended back to heaven in glory.

When the Holy Spirit is in you, rivers of life flow out from your innermost being. *"Jesus stood and cried, saying, If any man thirst, let him come unto me, and drink. He that believeth on me, as the scripture hath said, out of his belly shall flow rivers of living water. (But this spake he of the Spirit, which they that believe on him should receive: for the Holy Ghost was not yet given; because that Jesus was not yet glorified)"* (John 7:37-39). Not just a trickle or a cupful, not even a well you have to pump, but *rivers* of living water will bubble out from within you like an artesian spring!

Jesus promised His disciples that the Holy Spirit who had been with them would one day be in them. That day arrived shortly after His ascension. *"And when the day of Pentecost was fully come, they were all with one accord in one place. And suddenly there came a sound from heaven as of a rushing mighty wind, and it filled all the house where they were sitting. And there appeared unto them cloven tongues like as of fire, and it sat upon each of them. And they were all filled with the Holy Ghost, and began to speak with other tongues, as the Spirit gave them utterance"* (Acts 2:1-4).

The Power Source

Those who don't believe that the baptism in the Holy Spirit is a second, separate experience from salvation erroneously teach that God's miraculous power ceased with the passing of the first apostles. They don't believe in the gifts of the Spirit, speaking in tongues, or casting out demons—nor living in victory over sickness, disease, and poverty. They believe that if you see any of these miracles occurring today that God Himself did in the Bible, it's the work of the devil. Something's wrong with this theology!

The Holy Spirit is the power Source! Reject Him, and you won't see miracles, healings, demons cast out, or speaking in tongues. Accept Him by receiving the baptism in the Holy Spirit, and you open yourself to God's supernatural power working in all these wonderful ways—but you must receive the Source in order to have His power!

A Separate Experience

The Bible makes it clear that the baptism in the Holy Spirit is a separate experience from salvation. The only way you can miss this is if you have some kind of religious prejudice against it. In Acts 8, Philip went to Samaria and preached Christ. Seeing the miracles he did, many believed and were water baptized (Acts 8:5-12). When the church in Jerusalem heard what had happened, they sent Peter and John to check it out. They arrived, saw those who had been saved, and then laid hands on them to receive the baptism in the Holy Spirit (Acts 8:14-17).

Some people assume, "You aren't really saved until you're baptized in the Holy Spirit!" Acts 8 soundly refutes this. The Samaritans had received God's Word, were born again, and had been water baptized. If they had died before being baptized in the Holy Spirit, they would've been ushered into the very presence of the Lord Himself. Salvation saves and the baptism in the Holy Spirit empowers!

Certain disciples at Ephesus also demonstrate this truth. *"And it came to pass, that, while Apollos was at Corinth, Paul having passed through the upper coasts came to Ephesus: and finding certain disciples, He said unto them, Have ye received the hem; and they spake with tongues, and*

ct Your World!

ive today can attest to this separate,
Spirit in their lives after salvation.
Christians in Western countries deny
y of believers in the rest of the world
in the Holy Spirit!

th America have experienced some
ve've seen in recent times. Miracles
nes sometimes number into the tens,
ds. The vast majority of believers
gs have received the baptism in the
tongues.

rist worldwide, the
are those who belie
ditional, denomi
e either stagna
d believers a
e effective ng? Are you
ncing kir you long to join the
d's ore among believers who

iem,

the Holy Ghost came on t
prophesied" (Acts 19:6).

Impa

Millions of people al
distinct work of the Holy
Although many born-again
this experience, the majorit
have welcomed the baptism

Africa, Asia, and Sou
of the greatest outpourings v
regularly happen and church
even hundreds, of thousand
involved in these outpouring
Holy Spirit with speaking in

Across the body of Ch
experiencing the most growth
in the Holy Spirit. Most tra
that fight against this gift hav
serious decline. Spirit-baptize
Christian life, doing most of th
the biggest impact for the adv

Do you want to be wh
hungry to experience exci
winning side? You'll fin
have been baptized in

Holy
not s
19:1

wer
disc
bap
hin
(A
cc
as
h
(

Chapter 3

The Full Package

Jesus often referred to the Holy Spirit as the "Comforter." He'll function in your life many different ways:

The Holy Spirit will abide with you forever. *"And I will pray the Father, and he shall give you another Comforter, that he may abide with you for ever"* (John 14:16). Wherever you go, whatever you do, God Himself will be with you!

The Holy Spirit will comfort you through challenges and difficulties. *"Who comforteth us in all our tribulation, that we may be able to comfort them which are in any trouble, by the comfort wherewith we ourselves are comforted of God"* (2 Cor. 1:4). He'll also enable you to minister God's comfort to others.

The Holy Spirit will be your Teacher. *"But the Comforter, which is the Holy Ghost, whom the Father will send in my name, he shall teach you all things, and bring all things to your remembrance, whatsoever I have said unto you"* (John 14:26). He'll also remind you of everything the Lord has said.

The Spirit of truth will testify to you of Jesus. *"But when the Comforter is come, whom I will send unto you from the Father, even the Spirit of truth, which proceedeth from the Father, he shall testify of me: And ye also shall bear witness, because ye have been with me from the beginning"* (John 15:26-27). He'll also help you bear witness of Jesus to others.

"It's Better That I Go!"

It's to your advantage that Jesus is in heaven and the Holy Spirit is on earth. *"Nevertheless I tell you the truth; It is expedient for you that I go away: for if I go not away, the Comforter will not come unto you; but if I depart, I will send him unto you"* (John 16:7). Jesus could only be in one place at a time when He walked the earth as a man. Now, through His Spirit, He can be with every believer all the time!

The Holy Spirit will convict and convince. *"And when he is come, he will reprove the world of sin, and of righteousness, and of judgment: Of sin, because they believe not on me; Of righteousness, because I go to my Father, and ye see me no more; Of judgment, because the prince of this world is judged"* (John 16:8-11). He convicts you of not trusting Jesus. He convinces you that you're righteous in Christ. And the devil, who constantly hurls condemnation and lies at you, is judged.

The Holy Spirit will guide you into all truth. *"I have yet many things to say unto you, but ye cannot bear them now. Howbeit when he, the Spirit of truth, is come, he will guide you into all truth: for he shall not speak of himself; but whatsoever he shall hear, that shall he speak: and he will shew you things to come"* (John 16:12-13). The Spirit of truth will progressively share Jesus' words with you as you're mature enough to handle them. He'll even reveal things yet to come!

The Holy Spirit will glorify Jesus. *"He shall glorify me: for he shall receive of mine, and shall shew it unto you"* (John 16:14). He'll receive things from the Lord and show them to you!

God's power will flood into you as you're baptized in Him! *"But ye shall receive power, after that the Holy Ghost is come upon you: and ye shall be witnesses unto me both in Jerusalem, and in all Judaea, and in Samaria, and unto the uttermost part of the earth"* (Acts 1:8). Wherever you go, you'll be an effective witness!

Essential, Not Optional!

In light of all these awesome benefits, I urge you to accept the fact that the baptism in the Holy Spirit is not merely optional but essential. Receive His power so you can fully experience the Comforter!

The baptism in the Holy Spirit makes God's power available to you. Although you're not automatically transformed into a victorious Christian, you'll experience increasing victory as you draw out His power by faith. This is why some people who have received the baptism in the Holy Spirit don't exhibit more victory in their lives. God's power is available to them, but they haven't drawn it out. Those who reject the baptism in the Holy Spirit deny themselves access to His power. You must have received the Source in order to access His power!

Some Christians may have been baptized in the Holy Spirit without realizing it. They are wonderful people who don't speak in tongues or believe in a distinct experience with the Holy Spirit, yet they clearly exhibit all of the other characteristics of someone who has received the baptism. Often, with many of them, there was a time in their lives when they came to the end of themselves. They cried out to the Lord for help, asking for more of Him. After yielding, they had a miraculous encounter with God. Now whether they're aware of what they received or not, if the encounter actually included being baptized in the Holy Spirit, they can now speak in tongues anytime they want just by exercising their faith to do so.

God intends for you to have His full package! Some theologians from the 1800s and early 1900s taught about a second, separate experience with the Lord but didn't teach on speaking in tongues. They believed there had to be an enduing of power from on high, but they failed to embrace the accompanying miracles. Why receive only part of God's gift? Why not receive it all? Your loving heavenly Father cared enough to give you the baptism in the Holy Spirit. Honor Him by receiving the full package!

Chapter 4

Receive Him Today

God wants you baptized in the Holy Spirit! His longing to fill, control, and empower you far surpasses your desire to be filled, controlled, and empowered. In fact, the Holy Spirit has been eagerly waiting for you to open your heart and invite Him in. If you're ready to ask in faith, why not receive Him today?

Some groups erroneously teach that you must "travail" and wait on God to receive this experience. They believe God will baptize you whenever He wants to, and you have no control over it. This idea is based upon a misinterpretation of Acts 1:4-5, *"And, being assembled together with them, commanded them that they should not depart from Jerusalem, but wait for the promise of the Father, which, saith he, ye have heard of me. For John truly baptized with water; but ye shall be baptized with the Holy Ghost not many days hence."*

Jesus commanded the disciples to wait for the baptism because the Holy Spirit had not yet been poured out upon the earth. *"And when the day of Pentecost was fully come, they were all with one accord in one place...And they were all filled with the Holy Ghost"* (Acts 2:1 and 4). Pentecost was God's appointed time to pour out the Holy Spirit. Since He's already been given, there's no need to wait!

While seeking the baptism in the Holy Spirit, I was told I had to cleanse myself before I could receive. As instructed, I wrote out every sin I could think of on a couple of sheets of paper in my misguided effort to get "clean enough." Religious logic had deceived me into thinking "a jar full of rocks must be emptied before being filled with water" and "the Holy Spirit won't fill a dirty vessel!" Hogwash!

The baptism in the Holy Spirit is a *gift*, not something you can earn by travail or holiness (Luke 11:13). If you could rid yourself of all the sin in your life and be perfect before receiving the Holy Spirit, you wouldn't need Him! He's the One who will give you the power to be set free from lusts, habits, addictions, and desires. You can be delivered from anything when you receive and draw on the power of the Holy Spirit!

Wholehearted Desire

You need to desire the baptism in the Holy Spirit wholeheartedly. If you are persuaded and hungry, receiving can be as simple as praying a prayer. However, some people have been led to do so before they were really ready. Occasionally, someone needs a period of time to grow in their hunger and desire to receive. Where are you today? Are you persuaded and hungry for the baptism? Do you wholeheartedly desire to invite the Holy Spirit into your life?

Personally, I was desperate for the baptism in the Holy Spirit. I thought I had to pursue God and then wait for it. This misunderstanding only fed my growing hunger to receive. Then, when the baptism came, it was spectacular! Since this was something I'd longed for and sought after, I didn't just forget about it after speaking in tongues once or twice. Over the years, I've cherished this awesome gift from God. Without His power, I wouldn't be living in the victory and abundance I enjoy today—for which I'm eternally grateful!

Are you ready to commit yourself to the Holy Spirit without reservation? Are you hungry to receive God's power into your life? Perhaps you've even recited a prayer for this before but weren't really ready yet. However, after learning these truths—how you'll receive power, that this was something even Jesus had to have, that it totally transformed the apostles—you're ready to receive the baptism in the Holy Spirit.

Ask, Believe, and Receive!

God wants you filled, but you must reach out in faith to take it! *"For every one that asketh receiveth; and he that seeketh findeth; and to him that knocketh it shall be opened. If a son shall ask bread of any of you that is a father, will he give him a stone? or if he ask a fish, will he for a fish give him a serpent? Or if he shall ask an egg, will he offer him a scorpion? If ye then, being evil, know how to give good gifts unto your children: how much more shall your heavenly Father give the Holy Spirit to them that ask him?"* (Luke 11:10-13). How much more will your heavenly Father give the Holy Spirit to you! Ask, believe, and receive!

If you're ready, pray out loud the following prayer from your heart:

Father, I surrender to You completely. I recognize my need for Your power to live the Christian life. I'm hungry for You! Please baptize me in Your Holy Spirit!

By faith, I receive now the baptism in the Holy Spirit. I take it! It's mine in Jesus' name!

Father, thank You for giving me the Holy Spirit! Holy Spirit, thank You for coming. You are welcome in my life!

Continue to praise and thank the Lord for this wonderful gift. Take a few moments to enjoy His presence, and tell Him how much you love Him.

Some people have dramatic experiences receiving the Holy Spirit, and others are genuinely baptized without feeling a thing. One's not better than the other, as long as you received! Don't let outward manifestations, or a lack thereof, enable the devil to talk you out of this gift from God (Matt. 13:19).

If you believed in your heart when you prayed, then God's Word promises that you received. *"Therefore I say unto you, What things soever ye desire, when ye pray, believe that ye receive them, and ye shall have them"* (Mark 11:24). God always honors His Word. Believe it! As you stepped out in faith to obey the direct command of Jesus (John 20:22), you received the baptism in the Holy Spirit.

Congratulations—you've been filled with God's supernatural power! As you learn to tap into this power, your life will never be the same. For the rest of this book, I'm going to share about an important way you can draw His power out.

Chapter 5

Speaking in Tongues

God's Word reveals that speaking in tongues is one of the first manifestations to occur when you receive the baptism in the Holy Spirit.

Jesus' disciples spoke in tongues immediately after receiving the Holy Spirit. *"And when the day of Pentecost was fully come, they were all with one accord in one place. And suddenly there came a sound from heaven as of a rushing mighty wind, and it filled all the house where they were sitting. And there appeared unto them cloven tongues like as of fire, and it sat upon each of them. And they were all filled with the Holy Ghost, and began to speak with other tongues, as the Spirit gave them utterance"* (Acts 2:1-4).

As Peter preached the Gospel to the entire household of Cornelius, they received both salvation and the baptism in the Holy Spirit. *"While Peter yet spake these words, the Holy Ghost fell on all them which heard the word. And they of the circumcision which believed were astonished, as many as came with Peter, because that on the Gentiles also was poured out the gift of the Holy Ghost. For they heard them speak with tongues, and magnify God"* (Acts 10:44-46). Speaking in tongues was an outward evidence that these brand-new believers had truly received the Holy Spirit.

Peter used this fact to prove to the rest of the Jewish believers (who weren't there in person) that these Gentiles had indeed been born again. *"And as I began to speak, the Holy Ghost fell on them, as on us at the beginning. Then remembered I the word of the Lord, how that he said, John indeed baptized with water; but ye shall be baptized with the Holy Ghost. Forasmuch then as God gave them the like gift as he did unto us, who believed on the Lord Jesus Christ; what was I, that I could withstand God? When they heard these things, they held their peace, and glorified God, saying, Then hath God also to the Gentiles granted repentance unto life"* (Acts 11:15-18).

Paul ministered the baptism in the Holy Spirit to Apollos' converts in Ephesus. *"And when Paul had laid his hands upon them, the Holy Ghost came on them; and they spake with tongues, and prophesied"* (Acts 19:6). Speaking in tongues comes with the baptism in the Holy Spirit!

Every Spirit-Baptized Believer

Philip went down to Samaria and evangelized. Many people believed on Jesus when they heard his message and saw the miracles that he did (Acts 8:5-8). Later, Peter and John came to minister the baptism in the Holy Spirit (Acts 8:14-17). As the Samaritans began to receive, one of the new converts, who had been a professional sorcerer, saw them speaking in tongues and lusted for this power selfishly. Peter and John rebuked him for trying to buy God's gift (Acts 8:18-24).

Those who argue against speaking in tongues as initial evidence for the baptism in the Holy Spirit try to use Acts 8 to support their point. However, even though these scriptures don't directly say that the people of Samaria spoke in tongues, there's still plenty of evidence to imply it. Speaking in tongues is present every other time the Holy Spirit was poured out in the book of Acts. Also, this recently converted sorcerer *saw something* when the baptism was ministered, and it caused him to offer the apostles money in exchange for the supernatural ability to impart the Holy Spirit (verse 18). In order to maintain biblical consistency, this visible demonstration of power must have been speaking in tongues.

Speaking in tongues is an immediate audible manifestation of the Holy Spirit available to every Spirit-baptized believer. It's something you can do to help prove that you've received Him. However, tongues won't automatically force their way up out of your mouth just because you've been baptized. The Holy Spirit will never make you do something against your will. Therefore, you must choose to speak in tongues.

Darkness to Daylight

Personally, I stumbled into the baptism in the Holy Spirit. I had been seeking the Lord with all of my heart and crying out for Him to fill me with His power. On March 23, 1968, He dramatically answered my prayer by baptizing me in the Holy Spirit. At the time, I had no idea what this was because I'd never been taught about it. All I knew was that my intimate encounter with God had left me supernaturally empowered.

Revelation knowledge immediately began to flow. Before receiving the baptism in the Holy Spirit, I always had to trust what the preacher told me, and I assumed it was true. There wasn't any assurance in my heart or understanding of my own. I just followed their example and did what I was told. Then I received the Holy Spirit, and the One who had written the Bible started explaining it to me. He began revealing things to my heart. Instead of receiving information from the outside in, God Himself was teaching me from the inside out! John 14:26 describes this, *"But the Comforter, which is the Holy Ghost, whom the Father will send in my name, he shall teach you all things, and bring all things to your remembrance, whatsoever I have said unto you."* The difference was daylight and darkness!

In addition to revelation knowledge, I became bold and passionate for the Lord. God's awesome love and glorious presence constantly overwhelmed me. Witnessing to people changed from being a religious chore into a daily delight. The sick received healing when I prayed for them. However, these wonderful things combined to create some problems as well. For instance, my newfound zeal also got me kicked out of my church!

Religious Prejudice Overcome

Everything indicated that I had been baptized in the Holy Spirit, except I didn't speak in tongues. Why? I'd been taught against it! The church I was raised in didn't believe in the baptism in the Holy Spirit and thought that tongues were of the devil. Ignorance and wrong teaching predisposed me against this gift. Although speaking in tongues was available, negative feelings and fear prevented me from using it.

It took me a long time to renew my mind to what God's Word said about my new relationship with the Holy Spirit. Two and a half years after receiving the baptism, I discovered that speaking in tongues was a valid gift from God for today. Then another six months passed before I understood enough to yield to the Holy Spirit and actually speak in tongues. Until I saw what God's Word said about this, my faith wasn't strong enough to walk in it (Rom. 10:17).

If it weren't for my religious prejudice, I could have spoken in tongues as soon as I was baptized in the Holy Spirit. However, those thoughts kept me from enjoying God's gift, because their root was unbelief. Until I overcame them and brought myself to the point of voluntarily stepping out in faith, I couldn't speak in tongues. But as soon as I did, my life changed just as dramatically as when I first received the Holy Spirit!

You don't have to speak in tongues; you get to! Besides, there's really no good reason not to! Speaking in tongues releases God's power in your life, and it's available to every Christian who has received the baptism in the Holy Spirit. If you're not speaking in tongues, you're missing out!

Chapter 6

Proof for Today

God's Word clearly teaches that the gift of tongues is for today. This can best be seen in the three chapters of the Bible that deal specifically with the gifts of the Holy Spirit—1 Corinthians 12, 13, and 14. In addition to speaking in tongues, the other gifts are the word of wisdom, the word of knowledge, faith, gifts of healing, working of miracles, prophecy, discerning of spirits, and interpretation of tongues (1 Cor. 12:8-10). *(Although an exciting study in itself, further explanation of each individual gift is beyond the scope of our present purpose.)*

The local body at Corinth was one of the most carnal churches in the entire New Testament. A man had committed incest with his father's wife (1 Cor. 5:1). Believers were suing each other (1 Cor. 6:1 and 6-7). They divided themselves according to their favorite Bible teacher (1 Cor. 3:3-5). Gluttony and drunkenness characterized the Lord's Supper (1 Cor. 11:20-22). Tongues were being given in church services without interpretation (1 Cor. 14:26-28). Paul rebuked and corrected the Corinthians for all of this immaturity and sin.

These believers were carnal in spite of the gifts of the Spirit—not because of them! It's wrong to assume that the gifts are bad for you just because the Corinthians had so many problems. Actually, the opposite is true! Although maturity isn't instantly granted, the gifts of the Holy Spirit do promote spiritual growth. This is why three different times, Paul advised this carnal, sinful bunch to earnestly **"desire spiritual gifts"** (1 Cor. 12:31, **14:1**, 14:39). He knew the gifts would help them mature. That's good proof you should be speaking in tongues!

Whom Do You Believe?

I started talking about the Lord once to a woman whose house I was painting. When she asked me why I'd left the Baptist church, I told her that they kicked me out after I received the baptism in the Holy Spirit.

"Are you talking about speaking in tongues?" she inquired.

"Yes, that's part of it. I do speak in tongues, and that's why they asked me to leave the church."

She thought for a moment and then politely added, "Well, my church would have kicked you out too."

I asked, "Why would they do that?" and showed her 1 Corinthians 14:39. "The Bible clearly says here, *'Forbid not to speak with tongues.'*"

I've never forgotten her candid reply: "Well, there are lots of things in the Bible our church doesn't believe."

With that, I knew I couldn't minister to her anymore, because God's Word was not the final authority in her Christian life. She, like so many others, had chosen to believe her denomination's doctrines above God's Word. This is why 1 Corinthians 14 remains the most misunderstood passage of Scripture regarding the gifts of the Holy Spirit today.

Better with Love

The gifts of the Holy Spirit are meant to be operated in love. This explains why Paul wrote, *"But covet earnestly the best gifts: and yet shew I unto you a more excellent way"* (1 Cor. 12:31), as he launched into his famous love passage (1 Cor. 13). Some people have tried to say that love is the *more excellent way.* However, the context clearly shows that all of Paul's comments concerning love in chapter 13 pertain specifically to the use of the gifts of the Holy Spirit listed in chapter 12, and which are expounded on in chapter 14. His point is not that love is better than the gifts but rather that operating the gifts in love is better than using them without it.

The Holy Spirit doesn't control you like a puppet. He leads, guides, and inspires you to speak in tongues and operate the other gifts, but you are the one who actually does it. Therefore, it's possible to operate in the gifts carnally, make mistakes, and fail to be motivated by love. *"Though I speak with the tongues of men and of angels, and have not charity, I am become as sounding brass, or a tinkling cymbal. And though I have the gift of prophecy, and understand all mysteries, and all knowledge; and though I have all faith, so that I could remove mountains, and have not charity, I am nothing"* (1 Cor. 13:1-2). It doesn't matter which gift you're operating in—tongues, prophecy, faith—there's no benefit apart from the right motive. Therefore, let love motivate your use of every gift of the Spirit—including speaking in tongues!

In fact, God's love should be the motivation for everything you do. *"And though I bestow all my goods to feed the poor, and though I give my body to be burned, and have not charity, it profiteth me nothing"* (1 Cor. 13:3). Whether you attend church because you feel you have to or give into an offering out of sheer obligation, apart from love, it profits you nothing. From God's point of view, your motive is more important than your action.

Until That Which Is Perfect Is Come

People who reject the baptism in the Holy Spirit twist 1 Corinthians 13:8-10 in order to support their position that tongues passed away with the early church. *"Charity never faileth: but whether there be prophecies, they shall fail; whether there be tongues, they shall cease; whether there be knowledge, it shall vanish away. For we know in part, and we prophesy in part. But when that which is perfect is come, then that which is in part shall be done away"* (1 Cor. 13:8-10). They claim that God only gave the gifts of the Holy Spirit (speaking in tongues, prophecy, gifts of healing, working of miracles, etc.) to the early church because the Bible wasn't written yet. Asserting that the Bible is *"that which is perfect,"* they justify their conclusion that God doesn't do these things anymore. Nonsense!

If you read that passage in its context, you can easily see what it's really saying. Remember, Paul's subject for this entire section of Scripture (1 Cor. 12, 13, and 14) is to properly operate in the gifts of the Holy Spirit. He just finished saying that the gifts should be used in love (13:1-3). Verses 4-7 describe what that looks like. Then in verse 8, the Word states that when tongues cease, knowledge will too. Living in what's been popularly called "The Information Age," you and I both know that this hasn't happened yet. In fact, God's Word prophesies that in the end times, knowledge will greatly increase (Dan. 12:4).

"For we know in part, and we prophesy in part. But <u>when that which is perfect is come</u>, then that which is in part shall be done away. When I was a child, I spake as a child, I understood as a child, I thought as a child: but when I became a man, I put away childish things. For now we see through a glass, darkly; but <u>then</u> face to face: now I know in part; but <u>then</u> shall I know even as also I am known" (1 Cor. 13:9-12, emphasis mine). *"Then"* verse 12 refers to *"when that which is perfect is come."* At the time when that which is perfect is come, you will see Jesus face to face. Since that won't happen until the Lord's Second Coming or you die and go to be with Him, neither has tongues passed away yet.

"That which is perfect" refers to your glorified body, not the Bible. Yes, the Bible is perfect—inspired, inerrant, infallible—

but it's not what this phrase is pointing to. When you receive your glorified body, you will no longer see through a glass darkly or know in part. In your glorified body, you will see Jesus face to face and know Him even as He knows you—completely. For now, speaking in tongues has been given to help you grow in the knowledge of Him. In your glorified body, you won't need tongues or the other gifts of the Holy Spirit—prophecy, the word of wisdom, discerning of spirits, interpretation of tongues, etc.— to reveal the Lord anymore, because you'll already know Him fully.

The very scriptures people use to dismiss the gifts of the Holy Spirit actually prove their validity for today! As long as your knowledge of Him is incomplete, the gifts of the Spirit will function. Until you see Jesus face to face in your glorified body, you need to be speaking in tongues. Since that which is perfect has yet to come, God's miraculous power continues on earth today just as it did for the early church. You would have to already be corrupted with a predisposed, religious mindset in order to honestly look at these scriptures and interpret them as saying "God's miraculous power has passed away." *"Brethren, covet to prophesy, and forbid not to speak with tongues"* (1 Cor. 14:39)!

Miraculous Proof

Why do some people fight so hard against the truth that the baptism of the Holy Spirit and His miraculous power is for today?

96

Two main reasons are wrong teaching and a rejection of personal responsibility. Doctrines of men can render the Word of God ineffective. That's what happens when you hold on to religious tradition instead of God's Word (Mark 7:13). Also, there's a fear of having to produce biblical results. If you profess to believe in the baptism in the Holy Spirit, speaking in tongues, casting out demons, healing, and miracles, then that puts pressure on you to manifest them (Mark 16:17-18). Most people don't want to accept this kind of personal responsibility.

Instead, many hide behind a convenient theology. Calling themselves "Christian," they quickly confess that their sins are forgiven, while their lives offer very little proof. It's easy to profess, "My sins are forgiven," because you can't see a sin, and you can't see when it's forgiven. However, if miracles are really part of the Christian life, then there are things you can do to prove their reality. For instance, you can speak in tongues, cast a demon out, see blind eyes and deaf ears open, or even raise someone from the dead (I have personally done all of these things on multiple occasions and know many others who have done them as well— to God be the glory). In order to sit in front of the television living carnal, self-centered lives while defending their position of being forgiven, these people choose to believe only what God's Word says about forgiveness of sins while conveniently ignoring the rest. They may or may not truly be saved. Who would know?

Jesus used miracles to prove salvation. *"Whether is it easier to say to the sick of the palsy, Thy sins be forgiven thee; or to say, Arise, and take up thy bed, and walk? But that ye may know that the Son of man hath power on earth to forgive sins, (he saith to the sick of the palsy,) I say unto thee, Arise, and take up thy bed, and go thy way into thine house"* (Mark 2:9-11). Confronted by unbelieving religious leaders, Jesus asked them which would be harder to say, "Your sins are forgiven" or "Take up your bed and walk." No one can see a sin forgiven, but everyone in that crowded room, including the Pharisees, would be able to see if this man was healed or not. Either he would get up and walk, or Jesus' words would be totally violated. Therefore, "Take up your bed and walk" was definitely harder to say!

The people knew if Jesus could perform that which was hardest, surely He could do the least. *"And immediately he arose, took up the bed, and went forth before them all; insomuch that they were all amazed, and glorified God"* (Mark 2:12). Jesus used the fact that He could heal bodies and perform miracles in the physical realm to substantiate the fact that He could also do things, like forgiving sins, in the spiritual realm.

The reason many people hide behind this false doctrine that miracles passed away is so they can claim to be in relationship with God without ever doing anything to demonstrate it. That's just a convenient theology! The truth is that God still does miracles today, and you should be speaking in tongues until you receive your glorified body!

Chapter 7

Build Yourself Up

The primary purpose of speaking in tongues is to promote personal spiritual growth. *"For he that speaketh in an unknown tongue speaketh not unto men, but unto God: for no man understandeth him; howbeit in the spirit he speaketh mysteries... He that speaketh in an unknown tongue edifieth himself"* (1 Cor. 14:2 and 4). When you speak in tongues, you're building yourself up spiritually.

You also keep yourself in the love of God. *"But ye, beloved, building up yourselves on your most holy faith, praying in the Holy Ghost, Keep yourselves in the love of God, looking for the mercy of our Lord Jesus Christ unto eternal life"* (Jude 1:20-21). God's love for you never changes, but your experience of it does. Speaking in tongues helps you fulfill your responsibility to keep yourself aware of and enjoying God's unfailing love.

Speaking in tongues produces rest and spiritual refreshment. *"For with stammering lips and another tongue will he speak to this people. To whom he said, This is the rest wherewith ye may cause the weary to rest; and this is the refreshing"* (Is. 28:11-12). Your spirit is the part of you where God lives. It's brand new, pure, righteous, and holy. When you pray in tongues, you release into your soul and body that rest and refreshment that's already in your spirit.

Personally, I encourage myself by speaking in tongues! Whenever I feel tired or discouraged, I pray in the spirit until rest and refreshment come. Despite negative circumstances and emotions, I'll exercise my faith to pray in tongues until I'm aware of and enjoying God's love again.

Once you realize you can pray in the spirit anytime you choose, you have no excuse to ever be depressed again!

Praying Perfectly

When you pray in tongues, your natural mind doesn't understand. *"For if I pray in an unknown tongue, my spirit prayeth, but my understanding is unfruitful"* (1 Cor. 14:14). Unless there's an interpretation, your intellect doesn't know what your spirit is praying.

Your spirit has the mind of Christ. *"For who hath known the mind of the Lord, that he may instruct him? But we have the mind of Christ"* (1 Cor. 2:16). Your spirit knows all things. *"But ye have an unction from the Holy One, and ye know all things"* (1 John 2:20). *"And have put on the new man, which is renewed in knowledge after the image of him that created him"* (Col. 3:10). Therefore, your spirit always knows how to pray perfectly for situations, yourself, and others.

There's a big difference between praying from your spirit and praying from your mind. Your natural mind typically has incomplete information. It lacks full knowledge of God's Word, the situation, and the people involved. Therefore, you cannot pray from your intellect with completeness and one hundred percent accuracy. However, since your born-again spirit knows all things, it's impossible to pray in tongues without praying God's perfect will!

At times, the Holy Spirit may intercede for someone else through you as you pray in tongues. *"Likewise the Spirit also helpeth our infirmities: for we know not what we should pray for as we ought: but the Spirit itself maketh intercession for us with groanings which cannot be uttered. And he that searcheth the hearts knoweth what is the mind of the Spirit, because he maketh intercession for the saints according to the will of God"* (Rom. 8:26-27). This is especially helpful when your mind is not sure how to pray for a specific person or situation.

As you speak in tongues, you are speaking the hidden wisdom of God. Paul received the revelation for the messages he preached through speaking in tongues. *"Howbeit we speak wisdom among them that are perfect: yet not the wisdom of this world, nor of the princes of this world, that come to nought: But we speak the wisdom of God in a mystery, even the hidden wisdom, which God ordained before the world unto our glory"* (1 Cor. 2:6-7). *"For he that speaketh in an unknown tongue speaketh not unto men, but unto God: for no man understandeth him; howbeit in the spirit he speaketh mysteries"* (1 Cor. 14:2).

As Paul spoke God's mysteries in tongues, he built himself up spiritually and revelation knowledge came. As you pray in tongues, you'll be built up spiritually as revelation knowledge comes to you too!

Chapter 8

Interpretation

When you speak in tongues, you should believe God for the interpretation. *"Wherefore let him that speaketh in an unknown tongue pray that he may interpret"* (1 Cor. 14:13). It's beyond your carnal ability to grasp the mysteries and hidden wisdom of God that you're praying in the spirit. However, if you ask Him, God will supernaturally give you the interpretation.

The public use of the gift of tongues in a church service requires interpretation. *"If any man speak in an unknown tongue, let it be by two, or at the most by three, and that by course; and let one interpret. But if there be no interpreter, let him keep silence in the church; and let him speak to himself, and to God"* (1 Cor. 14:27-28). Without interpretation of a publicly given tongue, some people will think you're crazy. *"If therefore the whole church be come together into one place, and all speak with tongues, and there come in those that are unlearned, or unbelievers, will they not say that ye are mad?"* (1 Cor. 14:23).

Certain members of the body are given the vocation of interpretation for public purposes. *"Now ye are the body of Christ, and members in particular. And God hath set some in the church, first apostles, secondarily prophets, thirdly teachers, after that miracles, then gifts of healings, helps, governments, diversities of tongues. Are all apostles? are all prophets? are all teachers? are all workers of miracles? Have all the gifts of healing? do all speak with tongues? do all interpret?"* (1 Cor. 12:27-30).

Some people have misunderstood 1 Corinthians 12:29-30 to mean that not everyone should speak in tongues. However, Mark 16:17-18 states, *"And these signs shall follow them that believe; In my name shall they cast out devils; they shall speak with new tongues; They shall take up serpents; and if they drink any deadly thing, it shall not hurt them; they shall lay hands on the sick, and they shall recover."* Therefore, some have vocations of speaking and/or interpreting tongues given publicly in a church service, but every Spirit-baptized believer can pray in tongues for personal edification.

Of Men and Angels

Tongues come in two different types: tongues of men and tongues of angels: *"Though I speak with the tongues of men and of angels"* (1 Cor. 13:1).

Tongues of men are languages that either have been or are spoken on earth. When the disciples were first baptized in the Holy Spirit on Pentecost, they spoke in tongues of men (Acts 2:4-12). This wasn't merely a supernatural acceleration of language learning, because the speakers themselves had no idea what they were saying. The disciples didn't study all those different languages in the room they were in while waiting for the promise! The Holy Spirit suddenly baptized them, and their tongues became a supernatural sign to the unbelievers within earshot whose native languages the disciples were speaking (1 Cor. 14:22).

Tongues of angels are heavenly languages. Every Spirit-baptized believer can pray in the tongues of angels. When you speak mysteries and the hidden wisdom of God, you are speaking in an angelic tongue.

It doesn't matter if you speak in a tongue of men or an angelic tongue; you can ask God for the interpretation!

Light in My Closet

Learning to believe God for interpretation turned my life around! When I first prayed in tongues after being baptized in the Holy Spirit, I remember hearing God speak to me in my heart as revelation knowledge began to flow. However, when I started sharing what God had shown me in His Word, people criticized and informed me I was wrong, because they had never heard these truths before. Feeling isolated and alone, I really struggled with what others were telling me and what I was hearing in my heart. In the midst of all this, I just kept seeking the Lord.

For six months I meditated on God's Word all day long. As I wrote out hundreds of scriptures daily, I'd focus my attention on each individual word and phrase. After meditating this way for eight to ten hours, God's Word exploded with meaning in my heart, but my mind struggled to understand. So I'd shut myself in my closet to pray in the spirit for another hour or two. Sitting there underneath my clothes, I'd ask God to interpret to my natural understanding what I'd been studying. Then I'd pray in tongues for the purpose of personal edification.

At the end of that season, my trickle of revelation knowledge suddenly burst forth into a mighty rushing river! In fact, I received so much so fast that I finally told God I couldn't handle any more. It was just more than I could retain! Much of what I'm teaching today—over thirty-five years later—came as a result of what I learned at that time. I simply prayed in tongues and believed to interpret.

Gain Understanding

All you need to interpret tongues for personal edification is to gain understanding. When you're praying by yourself, you don't have to stop and get an interpretation in English. This method—praying out loud in tongues, then waiting until the English interpretation is given—works well in public, but it's not the only way to receive interpretation. You just need your mind to become fruitful.

God encouraged me through an experience that happened while I was still quite new at this. Since I'd been taught against tongues so strongly, I still wrestled with doubts about whether all my praying in the spirit was really beneficial or not. After spending two hours speaking in tongues one morning, someone whom I hadn't seen in four years showed up at my house. He knocked on the door, rushed in without greeting me, plopped down on my couch, and burst into tears. My first thought was, *I should have been praying in English instead of wasting all morning praying in tongues!* Then it dawned on me, *How would I have known to pray for this guy unless I had been praying in tongues?* My spirit had been praying perfectly!

All of a sudden, faith rose up inside as I stopped him mid-sentence, interrupting his blubbering attempt to explain the situation. By revelation knowledge, I finished describing the rest of his problem—and nailed it! This supernatural demonstration of God's power and love totally set him free! Through this, the Lord confirmed to me that I'd been praying in tongues for this situation earlier, and all I had to do was interpret. What I spoke to this man was the interpretation!

Mind Your Head!

When you pray in tongues, your mind can be occupied with something else. Since your spirit's praying and not your brain, your mind can wander. You can even think about things totally unrelated to God. That's why some people like to read the Word, enjoy godly music, or listen to Bible teaching while they pray in tongues. Others pray in the spirit while working, driving, or doing household chores. Personally, I've trained myself to pray with my understanding while praying in tongues.

When I'd pray in the spirit over longer periods of time, people whom I hadn't thought of in years would come to mind. At first, I just dismissed it, but when they'd suddenly call, send a letter, or even show up at my house—like that fellow did—I began realizing that God was giving me interpretations. They weren't always word for word, but also came as impressions, pictures, and unctions. As I recognized the Lord bringing these people to mind, I'd start praying for them. Then I'd follow through and see miracles happen every time!

God led me to call a good friend of mine one time after praying in tongues. We'd been out of touch with each other for several years. He answered the phone and immediately hung up on me. His reaction seemed strange since I knew God had prompted me to call. While sitting at my desk pondering this, the phone rang. Sure enough, it was my friend! He explained that he had just told God how he had spent his entire life ministering to others, but now that he was in need, nobody was ministering to him. My friend had barely finished praying "God, please send somebody to encourage me, or I'm going to quit the ministry!" when the phone rang and there I was. He was so startled, he hung up the receiver! This whole incident resulted from interpreting a tongue.

You can do this while praying for people, when you need wisdom for a challenging situation, or simply to understand a particular scripture. Just take the person, situation, or passage, and begin praying in tongues over it. As you're praying, ask the

Lord to show you what it means. Although understanding may not always come at that exact moment, God will give you an interpretation.

My friend prays in tongues over church services he's going to minister in. He prefers to receive the interpretation right away so he'll know in advance what God wants to do, who's going to be healed of what, etc. Personally, I don't always like to receive the interpretation right away. If God supernaturally told me what was going to happen at a church service a week away, my mind would try to analyze the situation and figure it all out in the meantime. I pray in tongues often without receiving anything from the Lord at that moment. However, when I need it a week or a month later, I'll ask God for the interpretation of what I've been praying in tongues. At that point, I receive exactly what I need from the Holy Spirit.

As you step out in faith to pray in tongues and believe God for the interpretation, you'll receive exactly what you need from the Holy Spirit too!

Chapter 9

Get Started

Speaking in tongues is not something you do just once to prove you've received the baptism in the Holy Spirit; it's a powerful tool to edify yourself spiritually. Whenever you pray in tongues, you cause yourself to rest, you build yourself up on your most holy faith, and you keep the love of God active and alive in your heart. As you speak forth hidden wisdom and believe for interpretation, revelation knowledge will open up and supply answers you couldn't get any other way. That's why the devil has fought so hard against this gift! He's afraid of what would happen if speaking in tongues ever became part of your daily Christian life.

The Holy Spirit inspires the words, but you have to say them. **"And they were all filled with the Holy Ghost, and began to speak with other tongues, as the Spirit gave them utterance"** (Acts 2:4). Notice that the Spirit gave them utterance. It's not just purely the Holy Spirit speaking through you. He gives you a prodding and a desire, but you must do the talking.

It's similar to how the gift of teaching works. If I stood before a group of people and prayed "God, please speak through

111

me, but don't let me say anything that's not of You" and then waited for Him to make me speak, I'd never say anything. It's my responsibility to step out in faith and start talking. God inspires the messages, but they come out through my personality, vocabulary, and mannerisms. God doesn't speak in Texas drawl; I do! The Holy Spirit supplies the content and I deliver it!

Fear short-circuits your ability to speak in tongues. You might have trouble at first, if you worry about it or try to analyze what you're saying. The Holy Spirit is inspiring you to speak, but it's your fear that's blocking it. Yield your tongue to the Holy Spirit, and then speak forth by faith the words He gives you.

Breakthrough!

I struggled to pray in tongues for months. Even though I was convinced it was of God and wanted it, I had a hard time receiving my prayer language.

A man came over to my house in an attempt to help me. He asked, "If you repeated something I said in Spanish, would you be speaking in Spanish?" I nodded. "Then if I spoke something in tongues and you repeated it, would you be speaking in tongues?"

"Yes, but I don't want to just repeat something; I want to speak in tongues on my own!" He kept insisting, so finally I gave in. However, I stopped after only getting through the first couple of words. Embarrassed, I told him I wasn't doing a very good job repeating what he said.

He argued, "Yeah, but you were speaking in tongues. That wasn't English!"

By then I had reached my limit. "No; I don't accept that. I wasn't speaking in tongues!" He just threw up his hands in frustration and left.

Immediately after this, I was on my way to minister to someone. In desperation I declared, "God, I'm just going to start talking. I believe that You are going to help me speak in tongues." Then I began making up nonsense words and saying them out loud. It seemed silly to me, so I didn't feel very good about it. However, I realized that I'd said two words that did sound pretty decent. Since they seemed like a real language to me, I figured they must be tongues. So I took those two words and started speaking them over and over again all the way to my destination.

Upon arrival, I experienced the best time of ministry I'd ever had before. I was convinced it was because I'd been praying in tongues. On my way home, I started praising God in the car and decided to pray using those two words some more, but I panicked when I couldn't remember them. After struggling so long to pray in tongues, I had forgotten the only two words I'd received!

Then I thought, *I'll just get another two!* So I started the process over again until another two words came. After using them for a while, I added a couple more. Within a few moments, I was speaking fluently in tongues!

Looking back, I know now that I could have spoken in tongues all along. However, I was under the false impression that the Holy Spirit would come upon me with such force that I wouldn't be able to keep myself from blurting out in tongues. When that never happened, I discovered He doesn't work that way. The Holy Spirit was just waiting for me to speak out in faith the words He'd been gently inspiring me to say.

Now it's your turn to do the same!

Let's Pray

"Father, thank You for baptizing me in the Holy Spirit! I'm so grateful You gave me this wonderful gift. Please help me to walk in all of its benefits!"

"Through speaking in tongues, I can draw on the power You've placed within me: for rest and refreshing, for building my faith and keeping myself in Your love, and for revelation knowledge as interpretation comes."

"I am a believer! Your Word says, 'These signs shall follow them that believe; In my name shall they cast out devils; they shall speak with new tongues' *(Mark 16:17). By faith, I will speak in tongues from this day forward, in Jesus' name. Amen!"*

Father Is Proud of You!

Now, by faith, say out loud those sounds coming up from

deep within. You'll be talking in a language unknown to you, but the Holy Spirit is the One inspiring it. You'll be speaking in tongues!

Go ahead—practice awhile! Enjoy yourself in the Lord!

If you aren't fluent right away, don't worry—God is proud of you! When little children start to speak, their parents know what they are trying to say. Even though it's baby talk, they're pleased. Your heavenly Father is proud of you, even if your tongue isn't fluent yet. If you'll just keep using it and not worry about yourself so much, tongues will begin to flow out of you unhindered!

As your brother in the Lord, I welcome you to the Spirit-filled life!

Receiving Jesus as your Savior

Choosing to receive Jesus Christ as your Lord and Savior is the most important decision you'll ever make!

God's Word promises *"that if thou shalt confess with thy mouth the Lord Jesus, and shalt believe in thine heart that God hath raised him from the dead, thou shalt be saved. For with the heart man believeth unto righteousness; and with the mouth confession is made unto salvation"* (Rom. 10:9-10). *"For whosoever shall call upon the name of the Lord shall be saved"* (Rom. 10:13).

By His grace, God has already done everything to provide salvation. Your part is simply to believe and receive.

Pray out loud, ***"Jesus, I confess that You are my Lord and Savior. I believe in my heart that God raised You from the dead. By faith in Your Word, I receive salvation now. Thank You for saving me!"***

The very moment you commit your life to Jesus Christ, the truth of His Word instantly comes to pass in your spirit. Now that you're born again, there's a brand-new you!

Receiving the Holy Spirit

As His child, your loving heavenly Father wants to give you the supernatural power you need to live this new life.

"For every one that asketh receiveth; and he that seeketh findeth; and to him that knocketh it shall be opened...how much more shall your heavenly Father give the Holy Spirit to them that ask him?" (Luke 11:10 and 13).

All you have to do is ask, believe, and receive!

Pray, ***"Father, I recognize my need for Your power to live this new life. Please fill me with Your Holy Spirit. By faith, I receive it right now! Thank You for baptizing me! Holy Spirit, You are welcome in my life!"***

Congratulations—now you're filled with God's supernatural power!

Some syllables from a language you don't recognize will rise up from your heart to your mouth (1 Cor 14:14). As you speak them out loud by faith, you're releasing God's power from within and building yourself up in the spirit (1 Cor14:4). You can do this whenever and wherever you like!

It doesn't really matter whether you felt anything or not when you prayed to receive the Lord and His Spirit. If you believed in your heart that you received, then God's Word promises you did. *"Therefore I say unto you, What things soever ye desire, when ye pray, believe that ye receive them, and ye shall have them"* (Mark 11:24). God always honors His Word. Believe it!

Please contact me and let me know that you've prayed to receive Jesus as your Savior or be filled with the Holy Spirit. I would like to rejoice with you and help you understand more fully what has taken place in your life. I'll send you a free gift that will help you understand and grow in your new relationship witht the Lord. *"Welcome to your new life!"*

Recommended Materials

Spirit, Soul & Body

Understanding the relationship of your spirit, soul, and body
is foundational to your Christian life. You will never truly
know how much God loves you or believe what His Word
says about you until you do. Learn how they're related and
how that knowledge will release the life of your spirit into
your body and soul. It may even explain why many things are
not working the way you had hoped.

Item Code: 1027-C   4-CD album
Item Code: 1027-D   As Seen On TV DVD album
Item Code: 318   Paperback
Item Code: 418   Study Guide
Item Code: 701   Spanish Paperback

Eternal Life

Is eternal life just about living forever, or could there be more?
What does God's Word say? Andrew's answer to this question
may change the way you view salvation and your approach
to your relationship with God. This single teaching is the first
from the *Introducing Discipleship Evangelism* album.

Item Code: DE01-C   Single CD

A Sure Foundation

God's Word is the only true foundation for your life. Listen as Andrew explains the supernatural process that occurs when you plant the Word in your heart. He uses the example of how Jesus dealt with John the Baptist's unbelief to reveal the power of the Word.

Item Code: 1034-C   4-CD album
Item Code: 1034-D   As Seen On TV DVD album

The True Nature of God

Are you confused about the nature of God? Is He the God of judgment found in the Old Testament or the God of mercy and grace found in the New Testament? Andrew's revelation on this subject will set you free and give you a confidence in your relationship with God like never before. This is truly nearly-too-good-to-be-true news.

Item Code: 1002-C   5-CD album
Item Code: 308   Paperback

You've Already Got It!

Are you trying to get the Lord to heal, bless, deliver, or prosper you? If so, stop it! God has already done all he will ever do for you. How can that be? Listen as Andrew teaches on the balance between grace and faith, and you'll understand you've already got what you need. Never again will you beg God for anything.

Item Code: 1033-C   6-CD album
Item Code: 320   Paperback

Introducing Discipleship Evangelism

Did God call us to make converts or disciples? It's an important question. The misunderstanding of that has led to some appalling statistics. Many evangelists now realize that only about 15 percent of those who accept Jesus continue in the faith. It's time we changed our thinking and started practicing what Jesus taught. Learn more in this enlightening series.

Item Code: 1028-C   3-CD album

Contact Information

Andrew Wommack Ministries
P.O. Box 3333
Colorado Springs, CO 80934
Helpline: 719-635-1111
www.awmi.net

Andrew Wommack Ministries Canada
P.O. Box 80010
Toronto, ON
M2J 0AJ

Andrew Wommack

For over four decades, Andrew has traveled America and the world teaching the truth of the Gospel. His profound revelation of the Word of God is taught with clarity and simplicity, emphasizing God's unconditional love and the balance between grace and faith. He reaches millions of people through the daily *Gospel Truth* radio and television programs, broadcast both domestically and internationally. He founded Charis Bible Schools in 1994 and has since established CBC extension schools in other major cities of America and around the world. Andrew has produced a library of teaching materials, available in print, audio, and visual formats. And, as it has been from the beginning, his ministry continues to distribute free audio materials to those who cannot afford them.